THE AYRSHIRE COLLECTION

Lendalfoot, looking towards Ailsa Craig

Alistair Keddie and Frank Beattie

Fort Publishing Ltd

First published in 2007 by Fort Publishing Ltd,
Old Belmont House, 12 Robsland Avenue, Ayr, KA7 2RW

© Photographs, Alistair Keddie, 2007
© Text, Frank Beattie, 2007

Thanks to the following organisations for access to their
properties and for permitting the reproduction of photographs:
Kelburn Castle; Palace Theatre, Kilmarnock; Communicado
Theatre Company; Loudoun Castle theme park; Landmark Trust
(Auchinleck House); Ayr Racecourse; Alloway parish church;
National Trust for Scotland (Culzean Castle); Blairquhan Castle.
Thanks also to Prestwick flying club and to the *Kilmarnock
Standard* for the photograph of Frank Beattie.

Typeset by Senga Fairgrieve

Graphic design by Mark Blackadder

Printed in Singapore by Imago

ISBN: 978-1-905769-09-4

Contents

Introduction

AYRSHIRE folk have much to be proud of. Their home county is the land of Wallace and Bruce, who fought for the independence of our nation. Even before their time it was at Largs that local people fought off the Vikings and sent *them* homeward to think again. Ayrshire is also the land of Robert Burns who taught us that no matter what our origins or beliefs, 'A man's a man for a' that,' words that echo across the centuries and are still relevant today. Ayrshire has produced many artists, writers, scientists, explorers and even builders of new nations.

Ayrshire is a small county in a small nation and yet the influence of people from Ayrshire can be found all over the world, particularly in Canada, the USA, Australia and New Zealand. So, before taking a pictorial tour of the landscape of rural and urban Ayrshire, let's take a brief look at the history of the county.

Geographically, Ayrshire is a county of sharp contrasts. There are hills and glens; rich agricultural land and rough moorland; golden sandy beaches and rough rocky shores. Ayrshire is a roughly crescent-shaped county, sometimes described as being rather like a huge amphitheatre with the hills to the north, east and south, and the land sweeping down to rich fertile plains along the river valleys to what we often call the sea. In reality it is still the Firth of Clyde.

No one knows for sure just when it was that the earliest settlers came to Ayrshire. It may have been at the end of the Ice Age, about ten thousand years ago. Presumably they came by boat. The areas inland consisted of deep, dark forests, which had an abundance of dangerous creatures such as wild boar or wolves, either of which might have thought that any stray man would do for a tasty treat. The human newcomers stayed close to the coast and built their communities there, living off the sea as much as the land.

Eventually, however, they explored inland and, at first, they did this by following the rivers. It is not known for sure when this happened. The earliest settlers have left very few remains, but it is now known that Ayrshire has had permanent settlements since at least 3500 BC. In any case, as soon as the earliest nomads arrived in what we now call Ayrshire, they started to change the landscape. Before the arrival of people the land had been shaped by nature. Scars from the time of glaciers can still be found in Ayrshire, as can the scars of an earlier time of volcanic activity.

As the new arrivals moved inland, these early Ayrshire folk made a greater impact on the landscape. They cut down trees for fuel and for building homes and boats. They cleared land for their dwellings and for growing crops. They domesticated animals and brought other farm animals into the area. They even made use of materials they found in the ground beneath their feet, such as clay, ironstone and coal. They built crannogs in wet moorland and in some of the area's bigger lochs. Other house builders constructed strong castles in places that allowed maximum defence. In some areas they drained the moorland to suit their agricultural needs. Whatever these early people did, they continued to change the landscape.

Ayrshire was created as a county in the twelfth century. Historians are not certain exactly when this happened but it was sometime between 1130 and 1150. The new county was split into three administrative areas: Kyle, Carrick and Cunninghame. By this time the land that had become Ayrshire was a vibrant place with hardworking people keeping a substantial number of communities going. There was trade with other countries and shipping was focused on the two main ports of Ayr and Irvine.

While the people of Ayrshire forged a new landscape, the landscape had a profound impact in making Ayrshire folk what they are. Ayrshire folk are fiercely independent and have a strong sense of moral justice. It was Ayrshire soldiers who helped win the battle of Largs in 1263, thus ending Norse interests in Scotland's islands. Perhaps it was pride in the heroes of that conflict that helped influence Wallace and Bruce, who in turn inspired the Covenanters to stand up to a king who wanted to exert his personal influence on the people through being able to rule the church.

The Covenanting movement was particularly strong in Ayrshire. And so it echoes down the years. In 1820, when the country was on the brink of revolution, Ayrshire men were ready to join the fight for justice and democracy. Remember, in 1820, any suggestion that ordinary men should be allowed to vote was likely to end in a one-way trip to Australia, or worse, to the gallows. During the long and, at times, bitter struggle to win the right to vote, Ayrshire men were in the fight, and in later years when women wanted to be part of the democratic process, Ayrshire women came to the fore.

Ayrshire has a proud military history and many Ayrshire men

fought with Wellington to hold back the march of Napoleon. It was Ayrshire man Charles Ewart who broke through the battle lines at Waterloo and seized the French standard, encouraging one side and demoralising the other. His tomb has a prominent place on the esplanade at Edinburgh Castle. Then in the twentieth century Ayrshire was one of the main training areas for the SAS, which was brought up to brigade strength early in 1944 in preparation for D-Day. This secret army trained in the hills, abseiled down tall buildings and pounded up and down Kilmarnock swimming pool, the only one in Britain with a wave-making machine.

In Ayrshire you will still find a wide variety of cottage crafts, but you will also find a good number of world-beating industries such as Johnnie Walker whisky, which was one of the first global brands. Ayrshire also has a rich agricultural heritage. Ayrshire cattle are known across the world and although potatoes were imported from the Americas, Ayrshire tatties are a national favourite. Ayrshire bacon is well known and so is Dunlop cheese. Ayrshire was once one of the foremost cheese-making areas in the country.

Ayrshire men, and women, have excelled in many fields. It was Captain Sandy Allan who pioneered passenger services across the Atlantic; Andrew Barclay's experiments helped make the Atlantic Telegraph possible; Alexander Fleming gave the world penicillin; Johnnie Walker gave the world his own blends of whisky. Cheers, Johnnie. Thomas Brisbane charted the night sky as seen from the southern hemisphere and gave his name to a great Australian city. Andrew Fisher became prime minister of Australia. John Witherspoon, once a Beith minister, became president of Princeton University and was a signatory of the United States Declaration of Independence.

Like Fisher, many other Ayrshire folk have left their mark on history. Scotland's railway revolution started in Kilmarnock with the Kilmarnock and Troon Railway. It was built between 1808 and 1812 to take coal from Kilmarnock to a new harbour at Troon.

Even before the line was completed it had a timetabled passenger service, one of the first in the world. It had a steam locomotive early in 1816, the first in Scotland. This, coupled with the need for engineering expertise in the coal mines, may have helped Ayrshire become a world-beater in a wide variety of heavy engineering.

Ayrshire folk have become great singers, actors and artists, writers and poets. Burns, of course, is known across the world. But other writers have left their mark. James Boswell, whose diaries recorded life in Scotland, London and other parts of Europe, was an Ayrshire man. John Galt and George Douglas Brown have left their mark in literature and so did poet Robert Service from Kilwinning, though he is better known in Canada than in Scotland.

The list of achievements of Ayrshire folk is endless. This book touches on many such aspects of Ayrshire life. It touches on the folk of the county, the industries, the towns and villages. If what they have achieved catches your interest, then go to your local library because the lives and work of many of these great people can be found in detail in other books. This is not their book.

There has never been an Ayrshire book like this one before. Ayrshire's natural charm and human history has not been fully explored before and, in this book, you will be able to see Ayrshire through the eyes of landscape photographer, Alistair Keddie. Alistair spent more than a year touring the county to capture the landscapes in each season, in all weathers and in many moods. He often returned to the same place many times, to get just the right shot. The result of all this effort is this collection of stunning pictures, a portrait of a county as we have rarely seen it before.

To go along with the pictures, local historian Frank Beattie has trawled through dozens of reference sources to tell something of the history of the areas that have been illustrated. This book is a blend of the work of these two experts.

Sit back now, and enjoy a tour through the history and landscape of Ayrshire.

Looking south from the Knock, which is a conical hill. The wonderful vista encompasses Largs, the island of Greater Cumbrae and, of course, the Firth of Cyde.

Knock Castle, bathed in a golden light. Two miles north of Largs, the castle, which dates from the 1850s, is a superb attempt by architect John Thomas Rochead to recapture an earlier baronial style. This building sits high on the raised beach and commands spectacular views of the Firth of Clyde.

Brisbane Glen. The power of nature can be seen in the hills above Largs. Some of them rise steeply and most have burns, which have eaten away at the surface. Between the hills there are valleys and glens, the most spectacular of which is Brisbane Glen.

A splendid view of Largs from Hailey Brae. In the background the ferry is leaving for Millport on Greater Cumbrae.

The Pencil. King Haco of Norway was worried by the restlessness in the western fringes of what he considered his domain. In 1263 he gathered a huge fleet off the east coast of Arran and set sail for Largs. But the day was won by the Scots under Alexander III and the defeat was devastating for the Norse interest in western Scotland. A tall, slender monument, The Pencil, erected in 1912, marks the site of the battle.

The origins of Kelburn Castle near Largs can be traced back to the thirteenth century and it is still home to the Earls of Glasgow. The grounds at Kelburn are open to the public in July and August when they are in full bloom. They contain many exotic plants and notable trees.

The gardens at Kelburn Castle are also home to the Clea burn, which tumbles into a hidden gorge.

The Three Sisters. As Ardneil Hill rolls down to the coast it begins to break up and from the sea it looks like three individual hills. These are the Three Sisters. The cliffs they present are popular with those experienced rock climbers who like a tough challenge.

Portencross Castle near West Kilbride was originally called Ardneil Castle and was owned by the Ross family, Sheriffs of Ayr. However, they supported Balliol and when Bruce became king of Scotland the castle was presented to the Boyds, the family that would later have a long association with Dean Castle in Kilmarnock. In 1588 ships of the Spanish armada hoped to find a safe refuge by sailing round Scotland. One ship was wrecked at Portencross and cannon were later recovered.

The island of Arran as dusk descends, viewed from Ardneil bay, which is just to the south of Portencross village.

Ayrshire has a rich agricultural heritage. In this scene Ayrshire tatties grow in fertile fields near West Kilbride.

Ardrossan Castle nestles on a hill overlooking the town. The castle was in English hands during the wars of independence. Before attacking it, Wallace set fire to a nearby house. English soldiers went to investigate and, while they were so doing, Wallace attacked the castle. In the seventeenth century much of the building was dismantled and the stone used by Cromwell to build a fort in Ayr.

The natural deep water at Ardrossan began to be developed as a harbour in 1806. At one time this was a busy port for all manner of cargo ships and later for pleasure cruisers. This ferry has just passed Horse island (in the centre, with tower) on its way to Ardrossan from Arran.

Kilbirnie Loch has been much altered since the days that there was a crannog here. Today its main supply of water is from the Maich Water. Water from Kilbirnie Loch runs north through various other small lochs and into the Clyde at Renfrew.

The massive DSM factory is the only large-scale producer of vitamin C in the Western world. Here it illuminates the night sky near Dalry.

A dead tree above Muirhead reservoir, which lies between Dalry and Largs.

Kilwinning Abbey. One of the finest ecclesiastical buildings in Scotland, the abbey's origins stretch back to 1187. Today the tower houses a heritage centre and it affords some fine views. Each June the abbey is home to a papingo shoot, in which archers attempt to shoot a wooden pigeon on top of the tower.

At one time Irvine was one of the busiest ports on the west coast of Scotland. Today the picturesque harbour caters mainly for small boats and pleasure craft.

The building that houses the Ship Inn on Irvine harbour-side is one of the oldest in the town. It was built in 1597. It is also the oldest pub in Irvine, having held a licence since 1754. Once the haunt of seamen, the Ship is now a popular family pub and restaurant.

A full moon rises over the Caledonian pulp mill. It is located on the western fringe of Shewalton moss, south of Irvine.

Dawn reveals the rugged beauty of Eaglesham moor in north Ayrshire.

M77. It took a determined and persistent campaign by local residents to have a motorway built between Kilmarnock and Glasgow. The road was opened in 2005 and has led to a dramatic improvement in safety standards.

Before 1643 Fenwick was part of the parish of Kilmarnock, but it was a long trek into the bigger town. Fenwick became an independent parish in 1643 when the village church was built. A fire in 1929 caused serious damage, but the character of the old building was restored.

The Jougs, Kilmaurs. Although this building is known locally as the Jougs, this simply refers to the iron neck-ring that was padlocked around the necks of criminals. The building was actually a tolbooth and court.

Dean Castle and the surrounding country park is the most popular attraction in the Kilmarnock area. The buildings are fourteenth and fifteenth century, with twentieth-century restoration of the ruin left after a fire in 1735. The castle is a museum with interesting collections of ancient musical instruments and armour.

Laigh West High church, Kilmarnock. A church may have been established in Kilmarnock in the earliest days of Christianity, though at that time there was probably no community. The first church was mostly for the use of wandering monks, who took the Christian message to anyone who would listen. It was dedicated to St Marnock and represented the beginnings of the town. A church still occupies the site today.

The Dick Institute, Kilmarnock. James and Robert Dick from Kilmarnock went into business using guttapercha for everything from golf balls to shoes and machine belts. They made a fortune and in 1901 James Dick provided the money for a cultural centre for his home town. The original suffered a devastating fire in 1909, but a new and bigger Dick Institute replaced it. It houses a library, art galleries and museum.

Kilmarnock railway station. Scotland's railway revolution started in Kilmarnock with the construction of the Kilmarnock and Troon Railway between 1808 and 1812. The line was also the first in Scotland on which a steam locomotive ran.

The view of the Palace Theatre and Grand Hall have been spoiled by modern road development. The magnificent Italian-style building was the work of architect James Ingram in 1863. Originally designed as Kilmarnock's civic centre, the buildings were home to the corn exchange, library, athenaeum, registrar's office, and the office of the inspector of nuisances. Today the buildings house the Palace Theatre and public halls.

Built in the 1730s the historic High Kirk of Kilmarnock is now the town's oldest church. Its kirk yard is the last resting place for many Kilmarnock notables, including John Wilson, printer of the Kilmarnock Edition of Robert Burns's poetry.

Looking north over Kilmarnock from the Bronze Age fort near the village of Craigie.

Loudoun Hill, which rises to 1,036 feet in the countryside near Darvel. William Wallace fought the English here and, in 1307, an army led by Robert the Bruce comprehensively defeated a much larger English force in the Battle of Loudoun Hill. The marvellous sculpture in the foreground is *Spirit of Scotland* by Richard Price and it commemorates Wallace.

Few towns in Ayrshire have had as much attention recently as Newmilns. Once an independent burgh, the people of the town felt they lost out when local-government services were centralised in Kilmarnock. But today the efforts of locals, the local authority and private developers to revamp the townscape is clear for all to see.

The remains of the nineteenth-century Loudoun Castle incorporated much of its fifteenth-century predecessor. The castle – which in its day was known as the 'Windsor of the north' – is a ruin that now sits in the midst of a family theme park with its various rides.

Poosie Nansie's, Mauchline. George Gibson was the landlord of this popular inn in the time of Burns and it was the setting for the 'Jolly Beggars'. Burns also used the characters he met there in his poems, including Gibson's wife, Agnes, whom Burns referred to as Poosie Nansie. The building is now a pub and museum.

The church at Mauchline is said to occupy a site used for religious purposes since the thirteenth century. The present building dates from 1829 and was designed by an amateur architect. Inside, the organ and stained-glass windows are worthy of note. In the graveyard you will find stones in memory of some of Burns's Mauchline cronies.

The Ballochmyle viaduct – built in the 1840s to carry the railway across the river Ayr – is one of the wonders of Victorian engineering. Located to the south of Mauchline it crosses the river in seven arches, all fashioned from local sandstone.

Catrine Voes. Catrine is a pleasant village that nestles on the banks of the river Ayr. The Catrine Voes were created as reservoirs to feed the local mill with water for power. Today they are wildlife sanctuaries managed by a local trust. These attractive wetlands are home to a wide variety of birds.

Parts of Sorn Castle go back to the fourteenth century and additions were made in later centuries. Like most of the residential castles of Ayrshire, the setting, on a bank of the river Ayr, is magnificent. The castle is open to the public for a few weeks in the summer and the grounds usually from April to October.

This obelisk on Airds Moss (close to the A70 near Muirkirk) commemorates those Covenanters who, in 1680, fought and died here in the cause of religious freedom. The memorial was erected in 1840.

Wallace's cave. Carved from solid sandstone – and spectacularly positioned overlooking the Lugar Water – William Wallace's hiding place can be found on the Auchinleck House estate.

The simple, yet elegant, Auchinleck House is the ancestral home of the Boswell family, which of course includes the great diarist and biographer, James Boswell. The present building was constructed for Lord Auchinleck around 1760 in the Classical style. It has been painstakingly restored by the Landmark Trust in recent years and is regularly open to the public.

ERECTED
IN MEMORY OF THOSE
WHO WORKED AND LOST THEIR LIVES
IN THE BARONY COLLIERY
1908 -- 1989

Memorial, Barony pit. When the coal industry was nationalised in 1947, forty-seven Ayrshire pits were taken into state ownership. A further nineteen were subsequently sunk. The Barony near Cumnock had four pits, with a peak workforce of 1,695. The old pit-head gear at the Barony is now a silent memorial to coal mining in Ayrshire.

The Square, Cumnock. The town's most famous son was James Keir Hardie, who founded the Labour Party. Cumnock is an old community and most of the buildings round the old market square were built in the eighteenth and nineteenth centuries.

Coal and iron made Muirkirk a thriving community. Now, however, the coal mining has ended. This memorial, to coal mining and coal miners, has a statue of a miner standing on a plinth. Around the plinth, in the style of a war memorial, are the names of seventy-seven local miners who died in accidents between 1892 and 1966.

With deep pits now a thing of the past Ayrshire's mining heritage is preserved by opencast coal mines, like this one near Cumnock.

Looking over Loch Doon to the lights of Ayr in the distance. Long and narrow in shape, Loch Doon, south of Dalmellington, is Ayrshire's biggest loch.

The former ironworks at Waterside village, also known as Dunaskin. It once employed two thousand men and was one of the finest examples of a Victorian ironworks. It later became a brickworks, then a museum, which has now closed.

The Wallace monument on Barnweil Hill, near Tarbolton. The name Barnweil is said to derive from a battle in which William Wallace set the barns of Ayr on fire ('the barns of Ayr burn weil'), killing many of the English soldiers who were inside. The monument was completed in 1855 and tens of thousands of people turned up for the opening ceremony.

Stair bridge, which was built around 1745. Historically, the Ayr is the most important river in the county and where it flows into the sea was recognised as a good place for a town long before the Romans arrived. Some of the best views of the Ayr are much further upstream, at places like Stair.

Stair Inn. This most attractive inn, which dates from 1820, was a popular halt for coaches throughout the nineteenth century.

Symington parish church. Built at the time of the Normans it is the oldest church in Ayrshire that is still in use today.

Sunset over the beach at Barassie, with the lights of Troon harbour and Arran on the horizon.

The Old Course, Royal Troon. The club was founded in 1878. One of Scotland's finest courses, and one of golf's hardest tests, Royal Troon has hosted the Open Championship on eight occasions.

There is a crescent moon above Arran as night falls on Troon bay.

A beautiful sunset over south bay, Troon.

Prestwick (officially Glasgow Prestwick) airport. The airport owes its origins to David F. McIntyre and the Duke of Hamilton, who were the first men to fly over Mount Everest. They used the fields at Prestwick for landing aircraft in the 1930s and worked tirelessly to establish the airport. Prestwick airport was the only place in the British Isles visited by Elvis Presley.

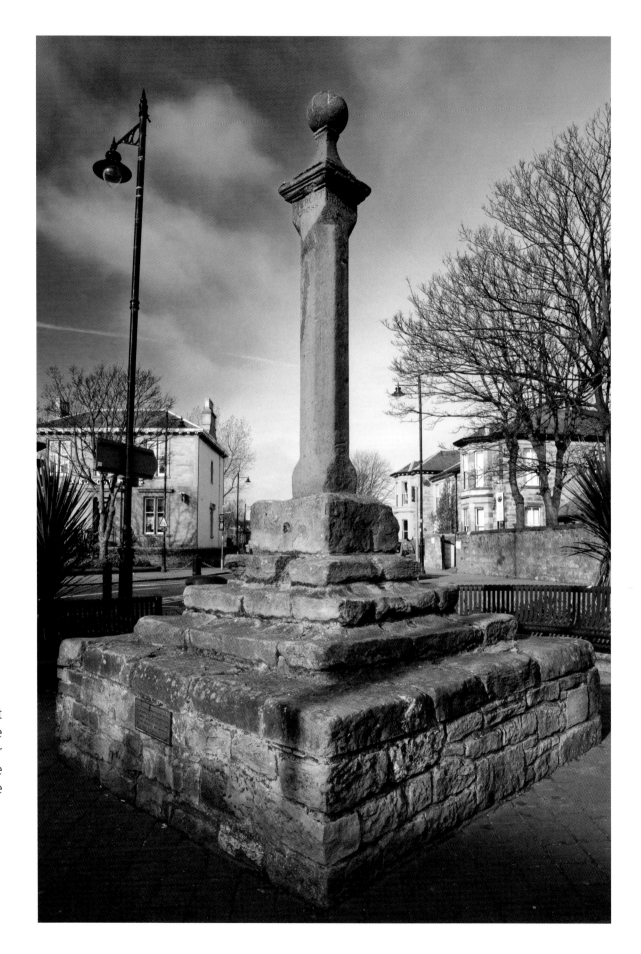

Prestwick has preserved its ancient mercat cross, even though the present version of 1777 no longer occupies its original site. This stone retains an earlier spelling of the town name: Prestick.

The base of this eighteenth-century windmill, close to Monkton, is known locally as the doocot.

The finishing line. A race at Ayr racecourse on Gold Cup day, September 2006. The Gold Cup meeting is Scotland's premier flat-racing event. Racing at Ayr goes far beyond 1770 when the town council approved plans for a course.

Gold Cup day is the highlight of the year for Scotland's racing aficionados. Ayr is about to undergo a major transformation that will confirm its place as the leading racecourse in Scotland and one of the finest in Britain.

The Auld Brig, Ayr, completed around 1470, and replacing an earlier wooden crossing. Had it not been made the subject of a famous poem, 'The Brigs of Ayr' by Robert Burns, it is likely that the Auld Brig would have been demolished.

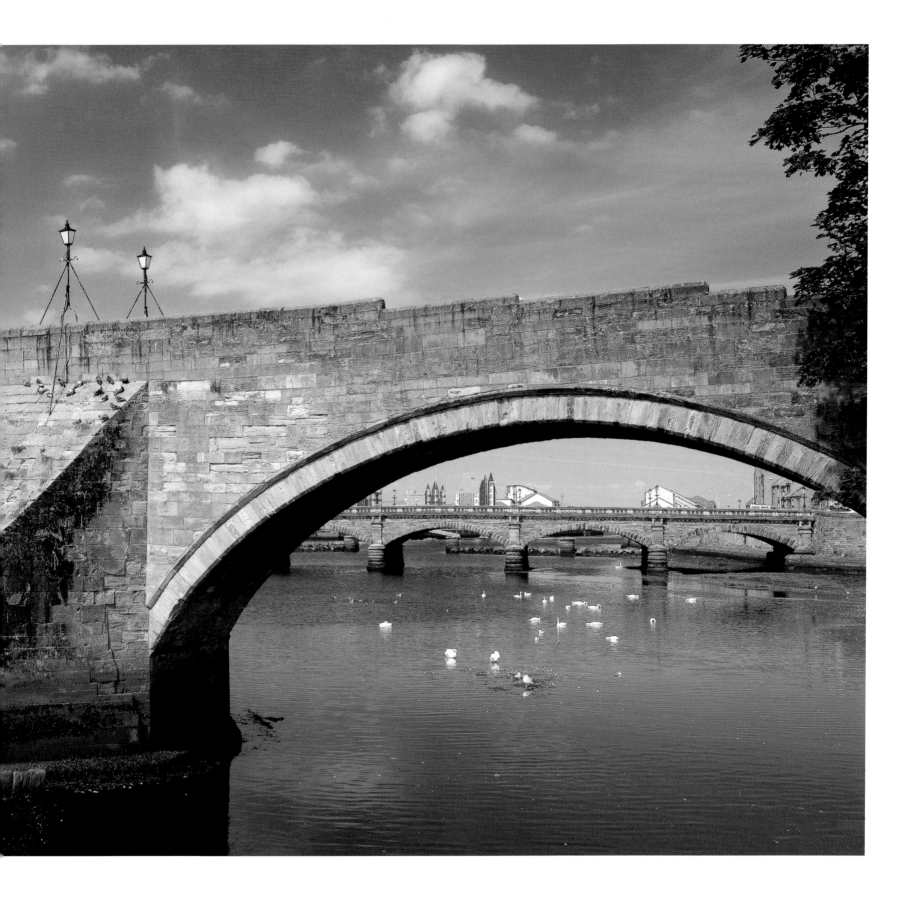

Ayr's New bridge, with the town hall in the background. Built in the late 1870s, this is the second bridge at this point on the river Ayr. The town hall dates from 1832 and its spire, at 217 feet, makes it the tallest building in Ayr.

St John's Tower, Ayr. The Scottish Parliament met at the Church of St John in 1315. It was later commandeered by Oliver Cromwell and incorporated into his fort. All that remains today of a once-extensive group of buildings is the tower. Some alterations were made to the tower, but it was restored to its former state in 1927.

Wellington Square, looking towards the Sheriff Court and the County Buildings. The square, perhaps the most elegant in the county, was developed in the early years of the nineteenth century and named for the Duke of Wellington, the victor of Waterloo. The façade in the centre is that of the court buildings.

The Fish Cross, High Street, Ayr at Christmas 2006. Although the original Fish Cross (which dates from the 1530s) has long gone the statue of the man holding the fish commemorates the fact that this was once the site of Ayr's most-important market.

The Church of St John the Baptist, also known as Ayr Auld Kirk. It was built in the 1650s to replace Ayr's original St John's church. A wonderful building, its graveyard is also fascinating to explore and friends of Burns, and many other local notables, are buried here.

Burns Statue Square. Known to Ayr residents as the 'top of the town'. The fine statue of Robert Burns was designed by George Lawson and unveiled in 1892.

The Tam o' Shanter Inn, High Street, Ayr. Named after the eponymous hero of Burns's epic poem *Tam o' Shanter*, the inn was built in the early nineteenth century. Notice the thatched roof and the rather attractive painting on the façade.

The floral displays in Ayr's Belleisle park are always a joy to behold.

Burns cottage, Alloway. Birthplace of the national bard this humble dwelling has iconic status not only for Ayrshire but also for Scotland. Built shortly before the 1759 birth of Robert Burns it attracts thousands of visitors every year.

Burnsiana:
Clockwise from top left:
'The Burns Memorial Window' in Alloway parish church, designed by Susan Bradbury; National Burns Monument, Mauchline; Burns Monument, Alloway; Alloway old kirk; house occupied by Burns in Mauchline; Bachelors' Club, Tarbolton.

The Brig o' Doon, Alloway. According to *Tam o' Shanter*, by Robert Burns, this is where Tam finally managed to escape the witches pursuing him. However, one of the harridans managed to pull off the tail from his grey mare as he crossed the bridge.

Ayr and the Firth of Clyde from Brown Carrick Hill in the Carrick Hills.

A beautiful sunset behind the island of Arran.

The photograph was taken on Ayr beach.

To the south of Ayr the ruin of Greenan Castle still guards the mouth of the river Doon. The original castle was built near the site of a motte and bailey, which marked the northern boundary of Carrick. Some historians now take the view that it was the site of King Arthur's Camelot.

The Heads of Ayr. Consisting of two cliffs that rise majestically from the sea the Heads of Ayr mark the southernmost limit of Ayr bay.

Dunure Castle. The small fishing village of Dunure is one of the most attractive, and historic, spots in Ayrshire. Although it is now a ruin the castle has witnessed the spilling of much blood down the centuries.

Croy Brae, or as it is better known, the Electric Brae. Motorists travelling west to east can see that they are driving down a gentle slope, but their vehicle struggles. Conversely, drivers travelling in the opposite direction can see that they are going uphill, yet the vehicle wants to freewheel. Hence the title, Electric Brae. It is of course all because of an optical illusion.

Maybole has been a burgh since 1516. The main street is dominated by Maybole Castle, which was originally built in 1620, apparently on the site of an earlier edifice. It was once much more extensive than now, but part of the old walled garden is extant.

These little mileposts may be unique to Ayrshire.

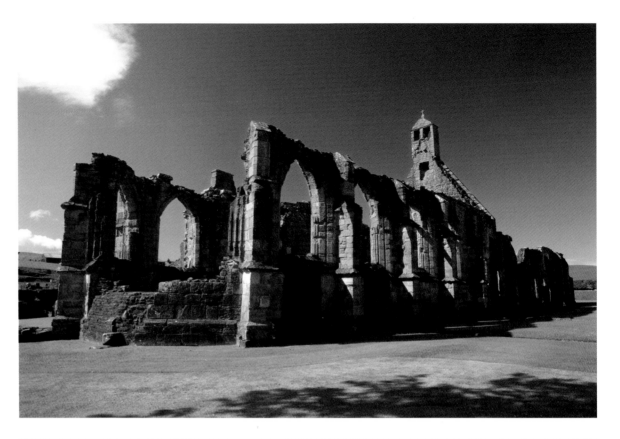

Crossraguel Abbey was founded in the thirteenth century by Duncan, Earl of Carrick and was run under the authority of the Paisley abbey. Today the remains are extensive and are open to the public. It was once a power base, which ruled over nine parishes of Carrick.

Maidens harbour. An old fishing boat lies at rest on the mudflats.

Culzean castle. The modern version of Culzean castle was designed by the eminent Scottish architect Robert Adam in the eighteenth century for David Kennedy, tenth Earl of Cassillis. It is considered Adam's masterpiece and today it is the jewel in the crown of the National Trust for Scotland. The castle houses important collections of arms and furniture and the associated buildings and grounds offer something for every visitor.

Swan pond, Culzean Castle. The delightful Swan pond was created in the early nineteenth century by the flooding of a wet meadow. The pond is a haven for an impressive variety of birdlife.

The gardens, Culzean Castle. The extensive gardens at Culzean are a source of pleasure for the thousands of people who visit every year.

The coast south of Maidens catches intense golden light from the setting sun.

Turnberry lighthouse, completed in 1873, was designed by Thomas Stevenson, the father of the great Scottish novelist Robert Louis Stevenson. It sits proudly on Turnberry Point facing Ailsa Craig.

Golf course, Turnberry Hotel. Turnberry was once home to an aerodrome and the landing strip runs through the golf course. Its fame as a golf centre is worldwide and Turnberry has hosted many major tournaments, including the Open Championship.

Kirkmichael parish church. This fine kirk was built in 1787, on a site that has been a centre of worship since the thirteenth century. The historic kirkyard has many interesting stones.

Blairquhan Castle, near Straiton, from 1824. This is one of the grandest houses in Ayrshire and is still a family residence. In the summer it is open to the public along with the walled garden and grounds.

The view from Craigengower Hill. Dawn lights the village of Straiton and the beautiful countryside.

Girvan is still a bustling fishing port and its harbour, at the mouth of the Water of Girvan, is one of the busiest in the county.

Ruined church, Old Dailly. The well-kept churchyard has a number of fascinating graves. There are also two lifting stones on the site, designed to test the strength of young men.

Sunset on Lendalfoot. The beauty of the Ayrshire coastline is vividly captured in this scene. Ailsa Craig can be seen in the background.

The castle and lighthouse on Ailsa Craig, against the backdrop of the Firth of Clyde. While the castle dates from the sixteenth century the lighthouse (another Stevenson-family design) was built in the 1880s following some disastrous shipwrecks.

Ailsa Craig from the east. This rocky outcrop has charmed locals and visitors for centuries. The poet John Keats visited Ayrshire in 1818 and was so taken with the island that he wrote a fine sonnet about it during a stay at the King's Arms in Girvan. Keats described Ailsa Craig as a 'craggy ocean-pyramid'.

Barestack cliffs, Ailsa Craig. Rising to 625 feet these are among the highest, and most spectacular, in Britain.

Sawney Bean's cave, between Lendalfoot and Ballantrae. The legend of Sawney Bean makes for a powerful story, so powerful that some claim it is true. It tells of a tribe of cannibals led by Sawney Bean, who lived in a cave and preyed on passers-by.

Ballantrae at day's end. The village is framed by Ailsa Craig to the west and Knockdolian Hill to the east.

From Ayrshire to Ireland. Sunset over the Firth of Clyde, with Ireland, the Mull of Kintyre and Ailsa Craig all visible from a vantage point near Finnarts bay.

Barr is a tiny village on the Water of Gregg in the picturesque Stinchar valley and an excellent starting point for walks in the forest areas of south Ayrshire.

The spectacular Stinchar Falls in the Carrick forest.

Winter on Loch Maberry, which impinges on both Ayrshire and Galloway. The broken ice produces an intriguing kaleidoscope.

Loch Dornal, which lies to the south-east of Barrhill village. In the distance snow-capped hills are visible.

Shalloch on Minnoch to the north-east of the Galloway Forest Park. At a height of 2,522 feet the summit of Shalloch on Minnoch is Ayrshire's highest point.

Ailsa abstract. The limpid beauty of this part of the Ayrshire coastline is abundantly clear from the beach at Maidens.

Two islands. It is fitting that the final page of this book includes both Ailsa and Arran. Both are indelibly associated with Ayrshire and in this scene they are perfectly framed by a magnificent cloud formation.